Smoking Pipes
of the North
American Indian

Smoking Pipes of the North American Indian

J.C.H. King

Published for
The Trustees of the British Museum by
British Museum Publications Limited

Front cover

Ha-na-tah-nu-muahk, Chief of the Mandans, with two calumets. From G. Catlin: *Souvenir of the North American Indians*. Before 1861, Vol. I, page 85.

© 1977, The Trustees of the British Museum
ISBN 0 7141 1547 9
Published by British Museum Publications Ltd
6 Bedford Square, London WC1B 3RA

British Library Cataloguing in Publication Data
King, J. C. H.
    Smoking pipes of the North American Indian.
    1. Tobacco-pipes   2. Indians of North
    America—Industries
I. Title
688'.4   E98.T6

Designed by Harry Green
Set in Plantin 10 on 12 and
printed in Great Britain by
Butler & Tanner Ltd, Frome and London

Contents

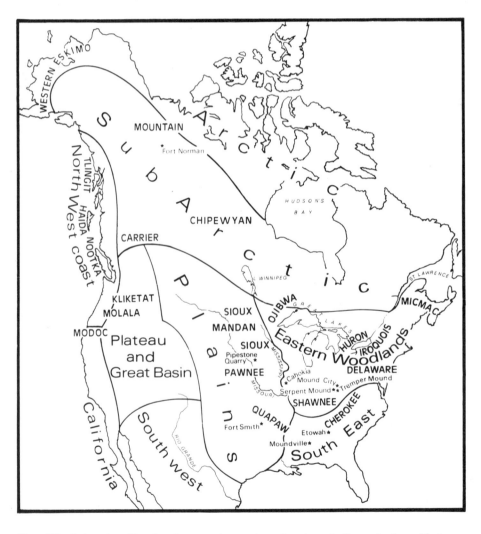

Map of North America with cultural areas and approximate locations of tribes at the time of first European contact.

Introduction

Of all the cultural traits of aboriginal North America, that of smoking tobacco was, perhaps, the most universal. In the middle of the nineteenth century almost every group of Indians used tobacco and its natural additives and substitutes. In most cultural areas, particularly in the Plains and Eastern Woodlands, pipe smoking was an ancient ritual complex. Among the prehistoric Hopewell of Ohio people of significance were buried with their pipes. The historic tribes smoked pipes, for instance, at ceremonies of healing, peace making, or at ceremonies connected with the hunting of the bison. In the North and Northwest, however, tobacco and smoking were largely introduced by European traders.

Pipe smoking is an idea central to the religious thought and behaviour of native North Americans. It is also, because of its religious importance, a way of approaching their technology, material culture and art. As elsewhere in the world, paraphernalia was highly embellished with skill and craftsmanship in North America. Therefore, using a category of objects such as tobacco pipes, it is possible to understand something of the craftsmanship of the original Americans.

Tobacco was consumed in a great variety of different ways and for different purposes. Sometimes it was smoked for pleasure, sometimes for health or for ceremonial reasons within a group of people. Tobacco was also used as an offering to the supernatural world. In ritual use the smoking of tobacco took the form of a presentation or gift as a means of approaching another person or the supernatural world. The communal smoking of tobacco also created a bond between a group of people involved, for instance in a ceremony preceding the hunting of bison. Tobacco could also be regarded as a bridge between the world of man and the world of the supernatural. In using this natural substance the user expected his supplication to God to be more effective. Tobacco was, nevertheless, always a common trade good and gift between people as well.

Indian tobacco smoking and the manufacture of pipes has one other important aspect: it was an essential area of contact between Indian and European. When the British first colonised Virginia in the seventeenth century, the growing of tobacco for the European market rapidly became of primary importance. Later, in the eighteenth and nineteenth centuries, tobacco became an article of trade and currency as Europeans explored further into the continent. The European acquisition of tobacco and the idea of pipe smoking symbolises, in a way, the colonisation of America. This idea, an almost sacred Indian trait, was taken out of context and copied to become merely a pleasurable habit.

Prehistoric North America

While the population of North America originally derived from Asia, many of the cultural traditions came from the South, particularly from Mexico. The most important introduction from Mexico was that of agriculture, which entered the American Southwest several thousand years before Christ. From the Southwest agriculture spread to the Mississippi river system, thus establishing the central areas of North America, until the sixteenth century, as the cultural centre of the continent. With agriculture, settled life began, leading to the growth of villages and eventually political organisations at larger than tribal level. Later, in the first half of the present millennium, Mexican forms of temples were built in the lower Mississippi valley; these were probably associated with Mexican forms of religion, and small states with socio-political structures similar to those found in parts of Mexico.

Agriculture did not spread over all of North America. The Arctic and Subarctic areas of Alaska and most of Canada are too cold to provide suitable conditions for farming. Before the arrival of Western settlers there was no farming on the high plains in California, the Great Basin, or along the Northwestern Coast.

With the farming of maize, beans and squash came the growing of tobacco. While tobacco was smoked throughout most of Mexico and North America, it became particularly significant in the central Mississippi, Missouri and Ohio valleys. There, as indicated by other innovations such as the burial of the dead in mounds, the cultural history of North America became distinct from that of Mexico. This cultural tradition, known as the Woodland tradition, arose in the first millennium BC. The stone tobacco pipes of the Adena and Hopewell are particularly associated with it. In the second half of the first millennium AD Mexican influences reasserted themselves; from this, the Mississippian tradition, come the large stone pipes associated with the Southeast. After the coming of Europeans from the sixteenth century onwards, smoking and the use of tobacco was taken by trade and conquest to the northern and western areas of North America. The Spanish introduction of the horse to the American Southwest stimulated the Plains cultures based on the hunting of the bison. With this florescence, from the eighteenth century onwards, the ritual use of pipes, associated with calumets (long stems with symbolical decoration), spread out over the central Plains of North America.

Smoking materials

Growing wild in North America are some fifty to seventy varieties of *Nicotiana*, the Latin name of the family of plants to which tobacco belongs. Of these at least eight species were smoked aboriginally and some of these were also cultivated.

The most common form of tobacco generally in use today is *Nicotiana tabacum*, but this was not native to North America. Instead it was probably introduced from Mexico at the time of the first European colonisation of the Eastern seaboard. At that time, over much of central and eastern North America, *Nicotiana rustica* was the species grown and used. In the Upper Missouri valley, and in some areas further west, *Nicotiana quadrivalvis* was grown and smoked. On the Northwest Coast among some tribes this species was cultivated for chewing. In many areas tobacco was not smoked by itself but was used with other vegetable matter. Sometimes this was to conserve tobacco, at other times, particularly after the introduction of the harsher tasting *Nicotiana tabacum*, it was to flavour the smoking material. A great variety of other materials were used, ranging from powdered wood in Alaska to dried willow bark and leaves in the Eastern Woodlands. These mixtures are known as *kinnikinnik*, which derives from an Algonquian word meaning mixed. One of the most common additives were the leaves of red-osier dogwood (*Cornus stolonifera*).

Forms and materials of pipes

Pipes varied as much as the materials used for smoking. Some were extremely impermanent such as the tubes of birch-bark used in the Northeast; others, particularly the stone prehistoric forms, were probably in use for several generations. The wide use of different minerals in prehistoric times suggests that the number of organic materials used was equally large. In historical accounts these raw materials include lobster claws in Maine, parts of gunstocks and barrels on the Northwest Coast, and a huge variety of decorative materials, both aboriginal and European in origin; most pipes were, however, made of stone. The terminology used to describe pipes is as varied as the forms. The simplest type is a smoking tube (95); these occur everywhere and although probably the earliest form of pipe, they continued to be made and used at least until the end of the nineteenth century. Pipes with the bowl at right angles to the stem are described as rectangular or elbow pipes; these also occur everywhere except for California and parts of the far West. Pipes with a flat base, whether the bowl is at one end or in the middle, are called monitor pipes, after the flat-bottomed warships used in river warfare during the American Civil War. Monitor pipes are usually found archaeologically, and then only from the central archaeological areas of the Mississippi–Ohio Valley, and the Southeast. Often, particularly with examples from the central riverine areas, the pipe bowl is in the form of a human effigy or an animal. From the central areas also come stone pipes too large to be portable; these are sometimes called effigy pipes if they represent animals, and idol calumets if they represent humans. Calumets is a term, derived from the Norman *chalumeau*, meaning reed, used to describe pipes of the Plains and Eastern Woodlands. The stems, rather than the pipe bowls, were associated with rituals of peace, war or hunting, and as such are often elaborately decorated with porcupine quillwork and feathers. Calumet is now used to describe the whole pipe and not merely the stem. Lastly the term

'Micmac' pipes is sometimes used to describe small pipes from the Northeastern areas and Northern Plains; these pipes usually are vase-shaped and set on a constricted stem with bar-shaped base. This form is found over a large area, and was made and used by many tribes other than the Micmac themselves; therefore the term is better avoided.

American Indian Pipes

Hopewell pipes of Ohio 100 BC–AD 200

The Hopewell people were agriculturalists who built great earthworks both for military and ceremonial purposes. The military or defensive earthworks were normally built on hill-tops and, although apparently fortified, were also probably used for ceremonial purposes. Ceremonial sites were mostly situated in the flat parts of valleys and were mainly religious and political centres. They took a variety of geometric shapes, particularly circles and rectangles, and often combinations of the two. The earthworks themselves were composed of banks up to sixteen feet in height, often broken by gaps probably used as entrances. Whereas the defensive earthworks sometimes included stone walls, the valley enclosures invariably used only earth. The ceremonial nature of the latter is suggested by the symbolical forms of the mounds and by the richness of the graves in burial mounds found within them. The Hopewell earthworks are not usually in the forms of animals; most of them are enclosures associated with burial mounds, some of them covering areas up to 100 acres. The most famous of the Hopewell sites are the Tremper, Mound City, Edwin Harness and Turner earthworks.

The Hopewell were agriculturalists who grew maize for subsistence, and tobacco. While a certain amount is known about their ceremonial life and mortuary practices from their earthworks, very little is known of their settlement patterns. It seems probable that they lived in dispersed, semi-permanent villages and that the earthworks were only used on special occasions. The mounds contained mortuary houses, wooden post buildings often containing several rooms each for a different purpose. The bones of the dead were brought to them after they had been denuded of flesh and they were usually cremated in shallow clay-lined pits. Grave offerings placed with human remains included objects made of a large number of exotic raw materials. Among these were mica from the Appalachian Mountains, grizzly bear teeth from the Rocky Mountains, conch shells from the coast of the Gulf of Mexico, and copper from the Upper Great Lakes. The artefacts found included mica sheets cut into the forms of hands, birds or human heads; large numbers of tools and weapons made of copper, flint and obsidian; polished stone objects such as *atlatls* or throwing-stick weights, and ear spools; engraved human and animal bones; caches of fresh water pearls, and monitor pipes often carved with an animal or human effigy. Two sites have yielded large numbers of monitor pipes: one is Mound City, excavated in 1846 by E. G. Squier and E. H. Davis; the other is the Tremper Mound, excavated in 1915 by W. C. Mills and H. Shetrone. Although the pipes in the British Museum come from Mound City a better general idea of a burial mound is provided by the Tremper Mound. It is oval and measures approximately 200 × 100 feet; attached to this oval were small additional mounds. The whole structure once covered a large mortuary chamber which had been burnt. It contained a number of clay pits for cremation, and other depressions designed as receptacles for the ashes. There were also rooms; one was probably used as a work or preparation room and another as a shrine. It was in the latter that the stone pipes were found, along with mica, bone, copper, pearl and other ornaments.

Mound City consists of a rectangular enclosure covering 13 acres. Within and around the earthwork are a number of mounds, many of which were excavated by Squier and Davis. Their greatest success came with the excavation of Mound 8 or the 'Mound of Pipes'. Here they found a very large number of pipes which had been damaged by heat and so, unlike many of those from the Tremper Mound, are in fragmentary condition. Along with the pipes were other grave goods, particularly a quantity of copper which had melted in the great heat of the fire. Mound City was badly damaged in the First World War by a nearby army training camp, and is therefore much restored. Most of the 200 pipes recovered from Mound 8 were in the form of animal effigies; a very few were carved with human heads, while some were plain. The pipes were made of hard flint clay, probably using copper tools. The rough form would have been cut out first and then the cavity and tube carved out. If this operation was successful then the pipe bowl could have been finished with an animal form. The most commonly represented effigies are those of birds (5–10), occasionally shown eating fishes (5). Other common forms show animals such as otters (3 and 14), wild cats (4 and 15), amphibians, including turtles, toads and frogs (1, 11 and 12), and small mammals such as squirrels (2). Almost invariably the head of the animal or human faces the smoker; very occasionally the head of the animal may face sideways (3). These pipes are undoubtedly the finest naturalistic carvings of prehistoric North America but their exact meaning and use will always remain unclear. It seems probable, by analogy with more recent cultures, that the animals carved on each one represent a symbol of a spirit personal to a particular human being or his family or clan. In the historical period among the Algonquian-speaking peoples of the Eastern Woodlands an individual might dream of an animal whose spirit would then protect him throughout the rest of his life.

Other types of pipe were carved by the Hopewell; the most spectacular are the large effigy pipes in the forms of animals, such as wolves. These pipes, often carved of steatite, usually weigh several pounds and would not have been carried about. They may therefore have been used in buildings reserved for ceremonial gatherings, and would have been used communally. Hopewell influences spread far outside the main Ohio area, and large effigy and monitor pipes continued to be made and used in other areas until historical times.

Stone pipes of the Mississippian tradition: 700–1700

In the second millennium the major cultural florescence of eastern North America took place in the Southeast, and is part of what is known as the Mississippian tradition. The Hopewell, characterised by the use of mounds and earthwork enclosures for burial, was a culture without obvious parallels in other parts of America. In Mexico, pre-Classic and Classic mounds, for instance, were used as platforms for temples and not for burials. The Mississippian tradition was, on the other hand, heavily influenced by Mexican cultures; particularly were mounds built as temple platforms. These were usually flat topped and rectangular and, sometimes, as in Mesoamerica, arranged around a plaza. In the period just prior to the arrival of Europeans some temple mounds reached enormous size. The great mound at Cahokia was enlarged to a height of around 100 feet with a base of 1000 by 650 feet; burial mounds were still built, although they are not so important at this time and, unlike the Hopewell, ceremonial sites were fortified. The people of Cahokia were maize farmers living in wattle and daub houses; their pottery was shell-tempered rather than grit-tempered as it had been with the Hopewell. Other contemporary important sites included Etowah in Georgia and Moundville in Alabama.

In the first years of contact with Europeans, the introduction of new diseases destroyed a large part of the population, probably causing some of the major sites to be abandoned before colonisation took place. It is therefore, often not possible to provide tribal or cultural attributions for pipes from other proto-historic cultures. One tradition of pipe making which continued from the Hopewell was that of making large heavy stone effigy pipes (16–18, 22). These often had conical

Hopewell pipe in the form of a young feline animal. (S) 271. Number 4.

Hopewell pipe in the form of a bird eating a fish. (S) 234. Number 5.

cavities in the top for the tobacco, with a second conical cavity for the entrance of the stem in the side. From this characteristic they are sometimes called biconical pipes. Large elbow pipes of square cross-section were also made with biconical tubes and cavities (23). In the central areas of the East Coast, simpler forms of portable stone pipes were made. Some of these related to earlier Hopewell derived forms, such as flat-based monitor pipes with the bowl at one end (21). Others had vase-shaped bowls (19), or bowls which were at right-angles to the stems; one characteristic features of proto-historical pipes of the Southeast is the addition of a rim to the top of the tobacco cavities (20, 21).

Early historical pipes of the Eastern Woodlands 1600–1870

The early historical Indian groups of the Eastern Woodlands subsisted on a mixture of farming squash beans and maize, hunting game animals and collecting plant foods. The proportion of farming to hunting and gathering varied considerably: in the Northeast among the Iroquois farming was much more important than it was, for instance, among the Ojibwa in the Western Great Lakes region. Tobacco was an adjunct to this economy, and usually grown rather than acquired by trade. The Iroquois sometimes grew tobacco in permanent beds; the plant was left to propagate itself, although it was manured. Alternatively, the tobacco seeds were scattered on the ground, since among some Iroquois groups there was a prohibition against its actual cultivation by turning the soil. The general uses of pipes and pipe ceremonials were probably of a similar kind in Northeast and east America as in the central areas. However, the ethnographic records of this period are very scanty: seventeenth-century descriptions of smoking usually concern relations between Europeans and Indians. Pipes were smoked during the Treaty of 1682 when the Delaware ceded land to William Penn for the founding of his colony; also tobacco and pipes were exchanged. On this occasion everybody, chiefs, other men and women, smoked a pipe during the negotiations. After the negotiations were completed everybody smoked again; each time a single pipe was used. Among the things provided by Penn were tobacco, pipes, and tobacco boxes. No pipe or calumet stems seem to have survived from the seventeenth and eighteenth centuries. James Ishan, an employee of the Hudson's Bay Company, in the 1740s commented that all trading negotiations were preceded by a ceremony of smoking, and illustrated a pipe of the type used in his diary. The stem was said to be six feet long, and to have been decorated with ribbons and feathers. The pipe that went with the stem was of a similar shape to that illustrated (39). Other eighteenth-century pipe stems are described in Sir Hans Sloane's catalogue of *Miscellanies:*

> 'A large calumet or tobacco pipe bole round made of black marble to which are fitted long pipes of reed or bored wood'. (24)

A Cherokee pipe is described as having a stem of 'cane coloured with spirrall red stripes'. Some calumet stems were obviously much more elaborate, and probably similar to those which have survived from the Plains from the early nineteenth century. Father Louis Hennepin described an Iroquois 'calumet of peace' in 1679:

'It is nothing else but a large Tobacco-Pipe made of Red, Black or White Marble: the Head is finely polish'd, and the Quill, which is commonly two feet and a half long, is made of a pretty strong Reed or Cane, adorn'd with Feathers of all Colours, interlac'd with Locks of Women's Hair. They tie to it two Wings of the most curious Birds they find, which makes their *Calumet* not much unlike *Mercury's* Wand, or that Staff Ambassadors did formerly carry when they went to treat of Peace. They sheath that Reed into the neck of Birds they call *Huars* [loons] which are as big as our Geese, and spotted with Black and White; or else of a sort of Ducks who make their Nests upon Trees, tho' Water be their ordinary element, and whose Feathers are of many different Colours. However every Nation adorns the *Calumet* as they think according to their own *Genius* and the Birds they have in their Country.'

Pipe stems were obviously not always as elaborate as this. Some (Plate 9) were quite plain, although they measured approximately eighteen inches in length. The bowls were usually simple, although they sometimes had crests or projections

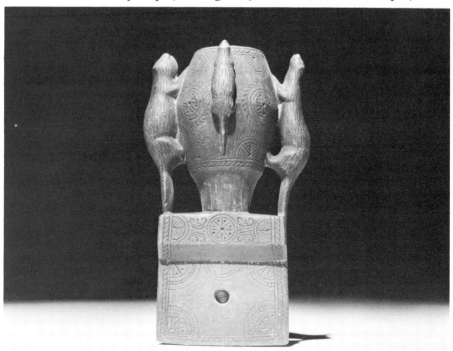

Micmac pipe bowl decorated with a beaver, otter and other animals. D.c. 13. Number 28.

to allow handling while being smoked. One common form of decorated bowl includes a dog or cat perched off the end of the bowl. Apart from the wooden one illustrated by Neander (Plate 9) and the stone pipe in the British Museum (27), there is another one in the Danish National Museum. Wood for bowls and stems and stone for bowls were not the only materials used for pipes in the seventeenth and eighteenth centuries. The Iroquois made and used pottery pipes in large quantities. These were often simple (30) with decorated or trumpet-shaped rims; sometimes they included effigies of humans and birds around the tobacco cavity.

In the nineteenth century pipes from the Northeast came, as elsewhere, to be made for souvenir purposes. The Micmac of Nova Scotia made finely carved small pipe bowls incorporating incised curvilinear designs. These were carved with figures of mammals such as deer, beaver and otters; animals of significance both ritually and economically (28, 31, Plates 10, 11). Micmac pipe stems were either wooden and decorated with incised designs, or as that presented to the Prince of Wales (later Edward VII) in 1860, completely plain. A more traditional form of decoration was to wrap the stem with coloured quillwork. In all cases the stems were relatively short. A variety of stone pipes were also made by the nineteenth century Iroquois. W. Bragge bought several souvenir pipes from the Iroquois at Caughnawaga which may have been types actually used (29), but he also bought examples carved of soft stone with multitudes of animals which are neither Indian in spirit or technique.

Nineteenth-century pipes of the Ojibwa of Minnesota and Ontario

The Ojibwa of Minnesota and Ontario are the most important Indian group living to the north and west of the Great Lakes between the Great Plains and the Subarctic. In the nineteenth century their subsistence depended largely on hunting for food and using their fur for trade; these included deer, caribou, moose and bears. Other food resources included fish in winter and collecting maple syrup as well as gathering wild rice and wild potatoes.

The Ojibwa beyond the northern and western ends of the Great Lakes held tobacco in great respect and made a variety of different kinds of pipe. Tobacco was a sacred material to be used in making requests to the spirit world because it came from the *manido*, the Great Spirit or god. Tobacco would be thrown onto the water by a man who, travelling in a canoe, feared a storm; it would likewise be thrown onto a fire by a man fearing a storm on land; tobacco was also used as an offering to features on the landscape such as rocks or waterfalls which were considered to be representatives of God. The Ojibwa in the nineteenth century used both native tobacco and trade tobacco. Because of its scarcity they added various other materials to it, particularly the leaves of the bear berry (*Arctostaphylos uva-ursi* (L) Spreng), the bark of the red willow (*Cornus stolonifera* Michx.) and of the spotted willow (*Cornus rugosa* Lam.). The inner bark of the last two was prepared by toasting it and then powdering it. In the nineteenth century only a very small proportion of trade tobacco would be used with the bark; by the early twentieth century this had increased among the Ojibwa of Minnesota to a ratio of two parts of bark to one of tobacco.

Smoking was a necessary activity for communicating with the supernatural; since supernatural help was necessary in treaties, it was essential for both parties to smoke during the negotiations. The Ojibwa's traditional enemies were the Sioux, and in the nineteenth century the initiation and ending of hostilities would have been accompanied by the smoking of pipes. Two chiefs, father and son both called Hole-in-the-Day, possessed a number of pipes which have survived. They came from Minnesota and were prominent in Ojibwa affairs until the 1860s. Hole-

Hole-in-the-Day. Photographed in Washington before 1865.

in-the-Day the older made attempts both to make permanent treaties with the Sioux, and on occasion, lead parties against the Sioux to take scalps. Hole-in-the-Day the younger was more peaceful, and in some ways assimilated himself into European-American society. He was quite successful in this for by the Treaty of 1855, when the Ojibwa were moved to northern reservations, he obtained a specific grant of land in his name. He was not, however, always at peace with the Sioux; on one occasion a party of Sioux desecrated his father's grave and in revenge he took six Sioux scalps. One of his pipes (32) has a scalp lock attached to it.

The stems of pipes from the Great Lakes area were not always long and elaborate; those for everyday use were short and cylindrical. The ceremonial ones were of two basic forms: they were either almost flat with a lens-shaped cross-section (35, 36), or cylindrical (32, 34, 44). Cylindrical wooden pipe stems wrapped with quillwork were made by many different groups, from the Micmac in Nova Scotia to the Mandan on the Upper Missouri. The Ojibwa made particularly elaborate cylindrical stems, decorating them with the characteristic black, orange, blue and white quillwork and also beads and hair tassels (44). More common than the highly decorated thin cylindrical stems are thicker stems with carved decoration, particularly in the form of cones and cylinders (32, 34). Another type of pipe stem which was favoured by the Ojibwa in the first half of the nineteenth century were 'puzzle' stems—stems with pierced designs made so as to confuse the beholder as to where the hole actually passed (35, 36). These stems were made of ash, or other wood with a pith centre; most of the non-'puzzle' pipes were made out of a central section of a branch. The pith down the centre of the piece of wood could be relatively easily removed with red hot wire, thus providing a tube without having to drill a hole. This could not, of course, be done with a 'puzzle' stem which had to be split open so that the crooked hole could be carved. Decoration for Ojibwa pipe stems included painting, and the attachment of ribbons as well as human scalp locks (35).

Many of the forms of pipes and stems of the Great Lakes are also common to the Eastern Plains tribes, particularly the Sioux. Pipe bowls used by the Ojibwa were sometimes very similar to those of the Eastern Plains. In particular Minnesota catlinite would be used and sometimes decorated with lead. The lead came from the allowances supplied by the United States government to the Ojibwa, under treaty, for making bullets. The more normal Ojibwa pipe bowls are of black stone, usually with a very simple rectangular form, and without any inlay (32, 34). Sometimes they have crests to the top and projections at the front; occasionally they have both. These projections enabled the pipes to be held, since they dispersed the heat generated while being used. Other decorative variations on the pipe bowl included inlaying with lead and catlinite (on a black stone bowl, 44), and lead inlay on a wooden pipe bowl (42). Spectacular pipe bowls were also made in the forms of human heads (38); usually the effigy on pipes of the Eastern Woodlands faced the smoker. A type of pipe often attributed to the Wyandot, a Huron

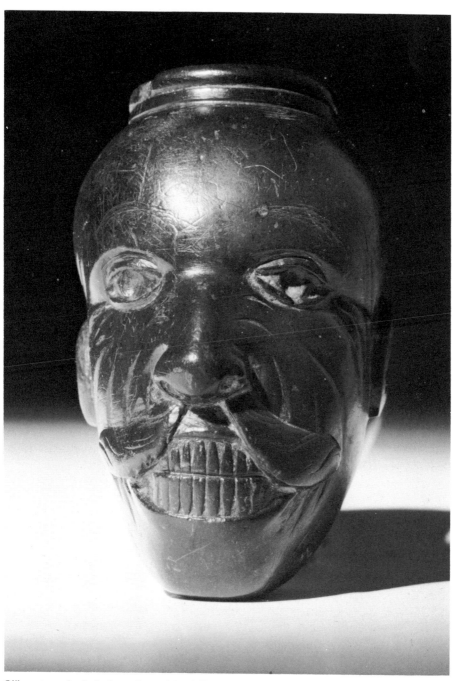

Ojibwa stone pipe in the form of a man's head. D.c. 40. Number 38.

group, is one in the form of a recumbent man holding a barrel and a glass. Other typical forms of pipes from the Great Lakes include bowls in the form of human heads, with both a crest and an anterior projection (40).

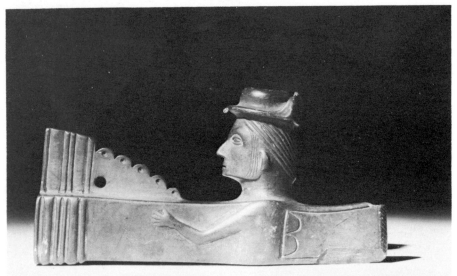

Ojibwa pipe bowl with the tobacco cavity in the form of a man wearing a hat. 1850.8–30.1. Number 40.

Wyandot pipe bowl in the form of a man holding a barrel, for alcohol, and a glass. 1949.Am.22.74. Number 37.

Nineteenth-century pipes and calumets of the Plains

The complex of ideas around pipes grew up in the central riverine areas of North America and remained most important among the people of the Upper Missouri, Plains and Great Lakes in the nineteenth century. The ritual surrounding the use of pipe calumets (stems) probably originated independently and only in relatively recent times has it become associated with smoking. By the nineteenth century the calumet or the reed was almost always associated with a pipe. Calumets were often objects of great religious symbolism, which varied from tribe to tribe. They were decorated with plaited porcupine quillwork, feathers and carving; the materials and symbols used were associated with ideas of the supernatural. Particularly important in calumet rituals was the antagonism between the sky spirits and the underwater spirits. The sky spirits are usually represented by thunderbirds (47–49), sometimes shown with lighting emerging from their heads. They usually have an hour-glass shape, while the underwater monsters are identifiable by their horns and long tails. In general Sioux calumets were a focus of tribal solidarity and power.

Woodpeckers were associated with both thunderbirds and calumets among the peoples of the Plains and Great Lakes. Pipe stems were decorated with the feathered skin of woodpeckers at the mouthpiece (49). One element of the symbolism connected with woodpeckers was that roaches, or small hair head-dresses, were thought to look like the crests on woodpeckers' heads. Feathered duck skin was also used to decorate pipe stems (54). In addition, feathers were sometimes

A thunderbird incorporated in the plaited porcupine quillwork decoration of a Sioux calumet stem. 1949. Am. 22.156. Number 47.

The Buffalo Dance. Mandan dance, preceding the hunt of bison, in which calumets were used. From G. Catlin: *North American Indian Portfolio*. London, 1844, Plate 8.

used grouped in a wing-shape so that when the calumet was being used in a dance it could be made to mimic the flight of a bird (43). These feathers were wrapped with quills, as were the stems of the pipes. Sometimes dyed hair would be bound onto the stem, usually near the middle where the quillwork ended. The most common form of quilled design was the wrapping of the stems with multicoloured plaited quills of changing colours: each additional strand would add more of the pattern (45–49). Quills were also wrapped onto pipe stems without being plaited, and occasionally simple geometric designs would be woven into quill wrapping along the stem (50). The most common colours for the quills before the introduction of aniline dyes were black, orange, white and blue. In the late nineteenth century much more varied colours were used, including different shades of violet, blue and brown (54); by that time other materials were being used to decorate pipe stems. These included inlaying pipe stems with stone and bone, wrapping the stem with copper wire, and adding small pieces of trade cloth decorated with beadwork (50). Another technique commonly used on the Plains, and elsewhere, was burning the stem to produce patterns; sometimes this was done with a red hot file (52). The Sioux carved their stems as well; like the peoples of the Great Lakes they made 'puzzle' pipes (51, 53), but usually the holes were quite simple. Designs were incised or carved in low relief, then painted (33), some stems were carved to form spirals (57). This was also done elsewhere on the Plains. The finest carving was reserved for the pipe bowls which, in the early nineteenth century, were very simple; they normally had a small anterior projection and a crest above the stem (43). The vast majority of pre-reservation pipe bowls are of this form. The first additional aspect of design was the use of lead, obtained from bullets, and used both as a means of mending pipe bowls and of decorating them (54, 55). First the bowl would be carved to its finished shape and the design engraved into the stone. The pipe was then wrapped with a durable material such as rawhide and the molten lead would then be run into the grooves. The designs used in the middle of the nineteenth century were relatively simple and geometric in form but by the end of the century they included figurative designs such as bison, dates and initials (54). Another aspect of this carving was the adornment of pipes with three-dimensional designs of significant animals such as bison or beaver (52 and 61). In the late nineteenth century, particularly after enforced settlement on reservations, pipes began to be made for souvenir purposes: most of them were in esoteric and non-traditional forms and were made out of catlinite. As elsewhere the clay pipe form was copied and adapted (59, 66).

Catlinite, like some other minerals used for pipes, is a red clay stone. It was mined from a quarry in Southwestern Minnesota in the territory of the Sioux who guarded it jealously and traded pipes to other tribes. When catlinite is first mined it is soft and so relatively easily worked. The Sioux used the fine purely red stone for their own pipes, and traded the less pure stone which often had white streaks to it. Although the majority of pipes from the eastern Plains are of catlinite other pipestones were used, some of which became black after they had

Yankton Sioux catlinite pipe bowl inlaid with lead. 1942. Am.7.1. Number 54.

Pawnee pipe bowl in the form of a woman faced by a man. D.c. 42. Number 58.

been worked and polished (58). Occasionally, the Sioux, like the Ojibwa, used black stone, and lead, as an inlay for red stone bowls (53).

Styles in the carving of pipe bowls are not always easy to distinguish, and tribal attributions are usually vague. Occasionally pipes were accessioned with their date of collection (60, collected in 1835); sometimes the place of collection is provided such as Fort Norman (56), thus suggesting that it is Quapaw. However, since pipes were traded and changed hands during war, this type of attribution is always uncertain.

Pipe tomahawks 1780–1900

These smoking pipes, although derived from Indian ideas, are almost always European or American in manufacture. From the sixteenth century onwards hatchet and axe blades were one of the most significant articles traded to Indians. As well as having purely practical purposes, particularly as weapons, they also had ritual functions which they took over from the aboriginal forms of tomahawks. One of these functions was the symbolic burying of a tomahawk when peace was made between two tribes of the Eastern Woodlands; when the word tomahawk came to describe hand axes or hatchets these were buried instead, from this comes the expression 'burying the hatchet'. Since pipes were used during the making of treaties, and as tomahawks were also significant then, it was a short step for a European trader, probably English, to think of combining these two ritual instruments into one article of trade. This probably happened in the early eighteenth century.

Pipe tomahawks could be made by any competent blacksmith; they could be manufactured from a simple piece of iron bent over to form a socket and the ends

Bear-in-the-Fork-of-a-Tree, Chief of the Sac and Fox, photographed with a pipe tomahawk in Washington before 1865.

would then be forged with a piece of steel to form the cutting edge. The poll of the axe would be pierced and fitted with a pipe bowl. Many of the latter pipe tomahawks were made in this way, but some of the earlier ones were manufactured in Europe. A very common early type has a blade of brass with a steel edge fitted into it; the blade is usually engraved with a floral design. This type was of English manufacture and is thought to be one of the forms used in the American War of Independence (65). Another similar type of British pipe tomahawk is sometimes associated with the War of 1812. One particular manufacturer, Holtzappfel & Co. (64), was a supplier to the Hudson's Bay Company. The stems or hafts would no doubt have been manufactured in America by the Indian to his own liking.

From at least the early part of the nineteenth century pipe tomahawks were favourite articles for presentation to important Indian chiefs by European and American politicians. Some examples were highly decorated, for instance with engravings of arms and of a European being threatened by an Indian, and with turned rather than carved stems. Some of the early pipes had bowls which screwed into the blade (62). By the middle of the nineteenth century pipes decorated with gold and silver were being produced for presentation to Indians. In the early nineteenth century the usage of pipe tomahawks began to change. Whereas originally they were hand and throwing weapons, as well as smoking pipes, in the nineteenth century they became more significant as pipes and symbols of authority. One aspect of this was the care spent on producing fine examples for presentation; another aspect was the production of pipes with less fine blades since they were not required for use. This may have been in part due to the increased availability of firearms, but it was also because as colonists moved west they came into contact with Plains tribes who preferred to retain their biconical stone clubs as fighting weapons. Although pipe tomahawks were traded to and used by Plains tribes, they were much more significant as a weapon in the Eastern Woodlands.

The most common type of blade for pipe tomahawks is that known as a half axe: it is a blade whose top edge is at right-angles to the handle or stem. Another early type of pipe tomahawk is that known as a spontoon tomahawk; these blades are in the form of a kite, and have curling flanges to either side of the blade. They derive from a type of hand weapon called an *espontoon*, a form of pole-axe used in the eighteenth century by commissioned officers. This type of pipe tomahawk may be French in origin (66, 67).

The last functional transition which pipe tomahawks went through is that common to many other types of pipe: they became objects specifically made as souvenirs. One of those illustrated (69) was said, at the time of its accession in 1900, to have been purchased from the Apache chief Geronimo while he was in exile in Florida. The stem is carved with alligators, and has few signs of use. Another type of late nineteenth-century souvenir pipe tomahawk was made by the Sioux. These involved the use of the red pipestone (catlinite). One such idea was to copy a whole pipe tomahawk in the stone (66). Another was to invert the idea of a red stone pipe bowl decorated with lead: a tomahawk blade would be fashioned roughly in stone and then encased in lead to give an impression of a pipe tomahawk of lead inlaid with stone.

In general, as with other pipes, pipe tomahawks are the product of the inter-action of European and Indian ideas. The form of the bowl in early pipe toma-hawks is probably copied from stone pipes of the Northeast; the axe is of course European. The whole idea, which began as a trade good made by Europeans for sale to Indians, inverted itself by the late nineteenth century to become an article which Indians on reservations made for sale to Americans. Equally, the decoration of the stems is a mixture of the different cultures. Quilled feathers for instance (67) and fur were both Indian decorative items added to pipe tomahawk stems; the stems were also decorated by burning. Sometimes it was done with hot iron files, on other occasions the stem would be wrapped with a coil of green bark and the whole stem passed through a fire to produce, in negative, a spiral pattern after the bark had been removed (65). European decorative ideas included wrapping the stem with copper wire and the addition of cut-out ornaments of sheet silver (68). As with other early Indian articles collected without any documentation it is usually impossible to tell which group favoured which form of pipe tomahawk. One type illustrated (68) is, however, a form that was particularly used by the Shawnee, perhaps because in the middle of the nineteenth century a local black-smith produced a quantity of this type while living near to them.

Pipes from the Northwest Coast

Alaska was first reached from the East in 1741 by a Russian expedition under Captain Vitus Bering. At that time none of the indigenous coastal peoples, from the Tlingit in Alaska to the Nootka in British Columbia, smoked tobacco. How-ever, both the Tlingit and Haida probably chewed a species of *Nicotiana*, perhaps *N. quadrivalvis* or *N. attenuata*, which they mixed with lime from burnt clam shells. Smoking other forms of tobacco, introduced by the European and Ameri-can traders and explorers in search of sea otter pelts and the Northwest Passage, began in the late eighteenth and early nineteenth centuries.

Northwest Coast society was hierarchical; chiefs and their families supported their claims to prominence through associating themselves with a vast mythologi-cal world filled with animals of divine and human attributes. These mythological characters, such as the raven and the wolf, and the myths in which they occur, were frequent subjects of the wooden carvings of the Northwest Coast. They in-clude totem poles, house posts and religious paraphernalia. It was natural, there-fore, that these ideas and motifs should be adapted for the new artefacts, smoking pipes. However, only a small percentage of surviving nineteenth-century Northwest Coast tobacco pipes were used by the people for smoking, since many of those made were used only as souvenirs for sale to Europeans. Most of these souvenir pipes were made by the Haida Indians of the Queen Charlotte Islands of argillite, a stone which is soft on excavation and so easily worked. Argillite is a form of carbonaceous shale found eight miles from Skidegate in the Queen Char-

Northwest Coast pipe bowl in the form of a whale chasing a seal. 1976. Am. 3.24. Number 72.

lotte Islands at a place called Slatechuck Mountain; only the Skidegate Eagle clan had rights of mining the argillite in the nineteenth century. It is not clear how or why the idea of carving pipes of argillite originated. However, the tradition of selling souvenirs to Western sailors was well established by the early nineteenth century; at that time, also, the trade in sea otter skins was declining and the Haida were no doubt anxious to find substitutes for trade in order to continue obtaining their supply of Western articles such as blankets, whiskey, tobacco and rice. The first forms of argillite pipe produced were probably roughly oval in shape and carved with mythological scenes (82): these would have begun being made in the 1820s. In the 1840s and 1850s new forms were created incorporating Western motifs; this idea may have originated with the copying of sailors scrimshaw. This would have coincided with the expansion of fur trading companies into what is now British Columbia (78–80, Plate 23). The most common subjects for these other pipes are sailors and ships' rigging and wheels (80), European-American houses, dogs and other animals (78, 79, 84). Some were made in the form of European clay pipes (83). Occasionally souvenir pipes were also made in wood, using the same non-traditional subjects (87, 91).

While the carving of pipes would not have been significant, economically, at the beginning of the century, the situation had changed totally by the end. During that time, the population of the Haida had declined from more than five thousand to less than a thousand. At the same time in the late nineteenth century many new forms of argillite souvenirs were made apart from pipes: these included model totem poles, figures of shamans, boxes, and large bowls. In the late eighteenth century, at the time of the first contact between Haida and Europeans, metal tools would not have been used for carving but by the beginning of the nineteenth century they had become relatively common, and argillite pipes were always made with iron tools.

While the Haida made souvenir pipes of esoteric form, all the peoples of the Northwest Coast made pipes for their own use; as with other elaborate Northwest Coast artefacts they were probably only used by people of prominence. Similar materials were used for these pipes, particularly stone and wood, but argillite was almost only used for souvenir pipes. The pipes used by the indigenous people were relatively simple and never used European motifs. Beavers (70, 86), ravens and mammals (90) occur used singly as the central form. Both types of pipe often in-

Nootka pipe bowl with the tobacco cavity in the form of storage box which is held by a woman. 1924.3. Number 74.

clude exotic materials as decoration. Particularly important was the *Haliotis* shell inlay (73, 81, 86, 88–90), usually traded from warmer waters to the south, and bone and ivory (89, 90). The more elaborate souvenir pipes incorporated quantities of these materials (78, 91, Plate 23). A significant use of elaborate materials was when parts of muskets were incorporated into indigenously used pipes (89). It is probable that gunstocks provided raw materials for pipe bowls, and gun barrels were certainly used as lining for tobacco cavities. It is very seldom possible to date the indigenous pipes because few were collected at the time of manufacture as they were intended for use. However, from the extreme care taken in the carving of the wooden ones, the wear and their patina, it is likely that most date from the early nineteenth century. The stone pipes of indigenous use are even harder to date, but probably derive from the same period.

The complicated nature and profusion of Northwest Coast pipes suggest something of the versatility of the people of the area. Not only were the Indians quick to adopt a habit which was brought by the Europeans, but they also invented new

Northwest Coast pipe bowl in the form of a beaver. 1949. Am.22.72. Number 86.

forms of pipes both for their own use and for trading back to the sailors and explorers. In particular, tobacco and pipe smoking on the Northwest Coast provides a sequence for the transformation of ideas. The idea of smoking was taken up by Europeans in the sixteenth century; for this purpose they adapted the Indian form of pipe for their own use. In the eighteenth or nineteenth century this idea was introduced to the Northwest Coast and there it was taken up and copies of the European clay pipes were made in argillite and wood (83–85, 87) for sale back to the Europeans.

Pipes of California and the Plateau

At the time of the first European contacts the natural resources in these two areas provided abundant subsistence from hunting and gathering activities. In the Plateau region this subsistence was based on salmon fishing by netting and spearing, and hunting animals such as deer; root and berry collecting provided further forms of food. Many of the basic forms of tobacco pipe in this area were derived from prototypes of the Great Plains (93). In the second half of the nineteenth century these pipes were decorated with lead and other white metals and were carved with rudimentary projections at the front. However, at the same time in adjacent areas other groups were still using the early prehistoric form of tobacco pipe, the tube (95). This was particularly true of California. The Californian Indians based their subsistence on gathering acorns in the interior valleys; hunting was also important, as was fishing and the collection of molluscs on the coast. Californian tribes used stone smoking tubes for healing as well as for ritual activities, blowing out smoke and inhaling air from the ill person to disperse the sickness.

Pipes of the Western Eskimo and Athabascans of the Western Subarctic

In Northwestern North America, eastern and western European colonists and traders met in the eighteenth century. During that century the Russians introduced tobacco smoking from the East to the continent from which it originated, and from which it had first been taken by Europeans two hundred and fifty years before. While the Russian forms of pipe copied by the Western Eskimo were of Siberian origin (99, 100) the Athabascans copied the European clay pipe form (97) and the simple rectangular pipe of the Plains (98). Both the Athabascans and the Eskimos were not originally tobacco smokers: the plant neither grew nor was it traded that far North aboriginally.

The Western Eskimo ivory pipe was manufactured in the nineteenth century particularly in the central Alaskan coastal area. Once again, as among the Haida, the pipes were especially made for trade to explorers, sailors on whaling vessels and administrators. The material was usually walrus tusk ivory, and the decoration was of three types. Either figures were carved in high relief on the top of the pipe; or else either geometric or figurative designs were carved on the sides of the bowl. Often combinations of these decorative techniques were used. The most common subjects for the figurative sculptural and engraved designs were subsis-

tence activities: hunting caribou from kayaks for instance (99). Other subjects included European ships and the building of dwellings. The bowls were made of
a variety of materials including copper.

The Athabascans, like the Western Eskimo, depended on hunting activities for
their subsistence, but lived in the vast areas of subarctic forest of Western Canada
and Alaska rather than the coastal areas inhabited by the Eskimo. Like other non-
smoking peoples when first contacted by Europeans they were amazed by these
people who could breathe smoke. In 1806 the explorer Simon Frazer met a group
of Carrier Indians in British Columbia. The Indians thought that the strangers
must be ghosts since from their mouth came the smoke with which they had been
cremated. The documentation for such pipes depends to a large extent on the
retention of the names of the places of collection: for instance, a specimen collected at Fort Norman (96), if of that area would have been made by the Mountain
Indians.

Collections of North American pipes in the British Museum
Most of the approximately 500 tobacco pipes from North America, come from
two collections, those of W. Bragge, and E. G. Squier and E. H. Davis. Bragge's
collection, containing about 160 North American pipes, was purchased in 1882
for the Christy Collection. Most of the pipes are undocumented, although Bragge
did purchase many of the pipes personally in and from America in the 1860s and
1870s. Bragge also commissioned G. Catlin to produce an elaborate manuscript
showing the forms and use of pipes in North America; this was probably executed
in 1864–6, and also came to the Christy Collection in 1882. Bragge included in
his collection watercolour and ink and wash drawings both of his pipes and of
pipes in other collections. Among the latter are a series of illustrations of the Hopewell pipes in the Squier and Davis Collection and also of fine pipes which he saw
in America.

Squier and Davis formed their collection of archaeological material from Ohio
in the 1840s. Their research was published in 1848 as the first volume of the Smith-
sonian Contributions to Knowledge. That institution, set up in 1846 by Act of
Congress under the will of an Englishman John Smithson, was unable to acquire
the collection when Davis came to dispose of it. As a result it was purchased by
Blackmore in 1864 and brought to Salisbury. When the Blackmore Museum was
broken up in 1931 the collections were divided between the British Museum and
a collector, H. Beasley. Most of the remaining archaeological material came to the
British Museum; however, the first curator of the Museum, E. T. Stevens, had
given away items to, for instance, W. Bragge and H. Christy.

The general ethnographical collections also contain pipes. Particularly important, but undocumented specimens, are in the Oldman Collection; the Christy
Collection contains a large number of pipes and also an interesting series of water-
colours of artefacts at the Great Exhibition of 1862; these include a number of
pipes from Canada.

Bibliography

Pictorial and manuscript sources in the Department of Ethnography

G. CATLIN. *Souvenir of the North American Indians.* 2 vols. Before 1861.

G. CATLIN. *A Selection of Indian Pipes in Catlin's North American Indian Collection.* 1852 or 1864–6.

C. N. KAUFMANN. *Changes in Haida Argillite Carvings, 1820–1910.* University of California, Los Angeles, Ph.D. thesis, 1969. Microfilm.

L. LEILA HAWKINS. *Illustrated Gleanings of Aboriginal Ornament from the International Exhibition of 1862.* 1862.

SIR HANS SLOANE. *Miscellanies.* Sir Hans Sloane's catalogue of his miscellaneous collections. Before 1753.

Publications relevant to the collections of tobacco pipes

M. BARBEAU. *Haida Myths illustrated in Argillite Carvings.* National Museum of Canada, Bulletin 127, Anthropological Series No. 32, Ottawa, 1953. (See 80)

T. BATEMAN. *Catalogue of Antiquities.* Bakewell, 1855. (See 39)

W. BRAGGE. *Bibliotheca Nicotiana.* Birmingham, 1880. (See 17–20, 23, 25, 27–29, 31, 32, 34–36, 38, 41, 42, 46, 49–52, 57–59, 61, 62, 64, 67, 68, 73, 75, 79, 80, 83, 87, 91, 97, 100)

H. J. BRAUNHOLTZ. *Sir Hans Sloane and Ethnography.* London, 1970. (See 26)

BRITISH MUSEUM. *Handbook to the Ethnographical Collections.* London, 1910. (See 75)

E. G. SQUIER and E. H. DAVIS. *Ancient Monuments of the Mississippi Valley.* New York, 1848. (See 1–16)

E. T. STEPHENS. *Flint Chips.* London, 1870. (See 1–16)

Other publications

J. E. BROOKS. *Tobacco; its history illustrated by the Books, Manuscripts and Engravings in the Library of George Arents junior.* New York, 4 vols. 1937–43.

JOSEPH D. MCGUIRE. 'Pipes and Smoking Customs of the American Aborigines', in *The Report for the U.S. National Museum* for 1897, pp. 351–645, Washington, D.C., 1899.

HAROLD L. PETERSON. 'American Indian Tomahawks', *Contributions from the Museum of the American Indian Heye Foundation*, Vol. XIX. New York, 1965.

GEORGE A. WEST. 'Tobacco, Pipes and Smoking Customs of the American Indians'. *Bulletin of the Public Museum of the City of Milwaukee*, Vol. XVII. Milwaukee, 1934.

Catalogue of Pipes

illustrated and referred to in the text

Cat. No.	Plate No.	Reg. No.	Description	Cultural and tribal or geographical location	Date	Collection
1	1	(S) 219	Red stone pipe: turtle. L. 7.25 cm.	Eastern Woodlands, Hopewell	100 BC–AD 200	W. Blackmore
2	1	(S) 259	Red stone pipe: rodent. L. 7 cm.	,,	,,	,,
3	1	(S) 269	Grey stone pipe: head of an otter. L. 9 cm.		,,	,,
4	1	(S) 271	Grey stone pipe: young feline animal. L. 8.75 cm.	,,		,,
5	1	(S) 234	Maroon stone pipe: bird eating a fish. L. 9 cm.	,,	,,	,,
6	2	(S) 231	Buff stone pipe: bird. L. 6 cm.	,,	,,	,,
7	2	(S) 230	Buff stone pipe: bird. L. 7 cm.	,,	,,	,,
8	2	(S) 240	Grey stone pipe: bird. L. 10.5 cm.	,,	,,	,,
9	2	(S) 225	Grey stone pipe: bird. L. 8 cm.	,,	,,	,,
10	2	(S) 228	Grey stone pipe: bird. L. 9 cm.	,,	,,	,,
11	3	(S) 224	Grey stone pipe: toad. L. 5.75 cm.	,,	,,	,,

Cat. No.	Plate No.	Reg. No.	Description	Cultural and tribal or geographical location	Date	Collection
12	3	(S) 218	Black stone pipe: head of a frog. L. 8 cm.	"	"	"
13	3	(S) 316	Black stone monitor pipe. L. 13.5 cm.		"	"
14	3	(S) 266	Red stone pipe: head of an otter. L. 9.5 cm.	"	"	"
15	3	(S) 274	Red brown stone pipe: young feline animal. L. 7.5 cm.	"	"	"
16	4	(S) 332	Black stone pipe: crouching man with a snake around his neck. H. 13.5 cm.	Eastern Woodlands, Ohio	—	"
17	4	D.b. 30	Orange stone pipe: frog. L. 13.5 cm.	Southeast, Kentucky	—	W. Bragge
18	5	D.b. 29	Black stone pipe: bird or turtle. L. 28 cm.	Southeast or Eastern Woodlands	—	"
19	6	D.b. 24	Black stone pipe: rudimentary face carved on the bowl. L. 13.5 cm.	Southeast, Lamar?	c. AD 1200–1300	
20	6	D.b. 26	Black stone pipe with lip to the bowl and two depressions along the stem. L. 13.5 cm.	Southeast, Tennesse	—	"
21	6	5218	Black stone monitor pipe with lip to the bowl. L. 20.5 cm.	Southeast	—	H. Christy
22	6	9856	Grey greenstone pipe: bird. L. 14 cm.	"	—	"
23	6	D.b. 22	Grey green stone pipe: rectangular cross-section. L. 14 cm.	Southeast, Virginia	—	W. Bragge
24	8	Sl. 1029	Black stone disc pipe bowl. L. 11.5 cm. D. 7.5 cm.	Eastern Woodlands	18th c.	Sir Hans Sloane
25	8	D.c. 43	Green stone pipe: bowl in form of two-faced human head. L. 13 cm.	Eastern Woodlands, New Jersey	17th c.	W. Bragge

Cat. No.	Plate No.	Reg. No.	Description	Cultural and tribal or geographical location	Date	Collection
26	8	Sl. 1214	Black stone pipe bowl with raised anterior projection. L. 20.5 cm.	Southeast, Cherokee	18th c.	Sir Hans Sloane
27	8	D.b.2	Black stone pipe with wolf or cat holding the bowl: finished in lead. H. 16.5 cm.	Eastern Woodlands	18th c.	W. Bragge
28	10	D.c. 13	Black stone pipe bowl decorated with incised circular designs and four mammals. H. 9.5 cm.	Eastern Woodlands, Micmac	c. 1860	,,
29	10	D.c. 22	White stone pipe bowl painted red. L. 8.5 cm.	Eastern Woodlands, Iroquois	c. 1860	,,
30	10	4353	Buff pottery pipe. L. 14.5 cm.	,,	17th c.	H. Christy
31	10	D.c.12	Black stone pipe bowl decorated with incised circular designs, deer's head, and beaver; wooden stem decorated with incised floral designs. L. 29 cm.	Eastern Woodlands, Micmac	c. 1860	W. Bragge
32	12	D.c. 34	Black stone pipe bowl; wooden stem carved with double cones and cylinders. Decorated with scalp lock tied with silk ribbon. L. 89 cm.	Eastern Woodlands, Ojibwa	c. 1840	,,
33	12	2564	Red stone pipe bowl inlaid with lead; the wooden 'puzzle' stem carved with geometric designs, painted red and green, wrapped with blue, orange and white quillwork. L. 91 cm.	Plains, Eastern Sioux	c. 1850	H. Christy
34	12	D.c. 82	Black stone pipe with a crest; wooden stem carved with cones. L. 82 cm.	Eastern Woodlands, Ojibwa	c. 1850	W. Bragge
35	12	D.c. 87	Red stone pipe bowl inlaid with lead; wooden 'puzzle' stem painted green, decorated with blue and green silk ribbons. L. 105.5 cm.	,,	c. 1840	,,
36	12	D.c. 84	Red stone pipe bowl inlaid with lead; a wooden 'puzzle' stem. L. 100.5 cm.	,,	c. 1840	,,
37	13	1949. Am. 22.74	Black stone pipe bowl: recumbent human holding a barrel and a glass. L. 11.5 cm.	Eastern Woodlands, Wyandot	19th c.	W. Oldman

Cat. No.	Plate No.	Reg. No.	Description	Cultural and tribal or geographical location	Date	Collection
38	13	D.c.40	Black stone pipe bowl: form of a human head. L. 13 cm.	Eastern Woodlands, Ojibwa	c.1860	W. Bragge
39	13	+6172	Brown stone pipe: bowl a human head, with a crest and anterior projection. L. 20 cm.	Eastern Woodlands	c.1850	H. Christy
40	13	1850.8-30.1	Green stone pipe: bowl a human wearing a European hat, with a crest and anterior projection. L. 16.75 cm.	,,	c.1840	Doubleday
41	13	D.c.38	Black stone pipe bowl: pierced projections. L. 15 cm.	Eastern Woodlands, Ojibwa	c.1850	W. Bragge
42	13	D.c.33	Wooden pipe bowl: with crest, inlaid with lead and varnished. L. 15.25 cm.	,,	c.1860	,,
43	14	5200	Red stone pipe bowl, wooden stem decorated in orange, black and white quillwork, and red dyed hair. With seven red dyed feathers wrapped with black and white quillwork and decorated with dyed hair. L. 113 cm.	Plains, Mandan?	c.1825	H. Christy
44	14	1921.10-14.107	Black stone pipe bowl inlaid with lead and red stone: wooden stem wrapped in orange, blue, black and white quillwork, decorated with hair tassels. The stem and bowl are joined with two plaited orange and white lengths of quillwork, decorated with a short length of blue and white beads. L. 79 cm.	Eastern Woodlands, Ojibwa	c.1840	Yorkshire Philosophical Society Museum
45	14	1893.10-24.1.	Red stone pipe bowl with vertical disc: wooden stem decorated in orange, blue, black and white quillwork. L. 103 cm.	Plains, Eastern Sioux	c.1840	H. Norris
46	15	D.c.85	Red stone pipe bowl: wooden stem decorated with orange, black, white and yellow quillwork, birdskin and dyed hair. L. 114 cm.	,,	c.1840	W. Bragge
47	15	1949. Am. 22.156	Wooden stem decorated with burnt file marks, orange, blue, black, white and yellow quillwork. L. 96 cm.	,,	c.1840	,,

Cat. No.	Plate No.	Reg. No.	Description	Cultural and tribal or geographical location	Date	Collection
48	15	1949. Am. 22.155	Wooden stem decorated with orange, blue, black and white quillwork and red dyed hair. L. 98.5 cm.	Plains, Eastern Sioux	c. 1840	W. Oldman
49	15	S. 771	Red stone pipe bowl: wooden stem, painted blue, decorated with orange, black and white quillwork, birdskin and dyed hair. L. 112 cm.	”	c. 1840	H. Christy
50	16	D.c. 83	Red stone pipe bowl inlaid with lead: wooden stem decorated with blue and red trade cloth, black and white beads, red, blue and white quillwork, birdskin and hair. L. 85 cm.	”	c. 1850	W. Bragge
51	16	D.c. 89	Red stone pipe bowl: wooden 'puzzle' stem decorated with orange, blue, black and white quillwork, and red dyed hair. L. 91 cm.	”	c. 1840	”
52	16	D.c. 86	Red stone pipe bowl carved with two bison: wooden stem decorated with bands of burnt file marks and dyed hair. L. 100.5 cm.	Plains, Pawnee?	c. 1860	”
53	16	2565	Red stone pipe bowl inlaid with black stone and lead: wooden 'puzzle' stem decorated with orange, blue and yellow quillwork, and dyed hair. L. 97.5 cm.	Plains, Eastern Sioux	c. 1850	H. Christy
54	17	1942. Am. 7.1	Red stone pipe bowl inlaid with lead: wooden stem decorated with red, green, yellow, brown and blue quillwork, birdskin and hair. L. 67 cm.	Plains, Sioux	c. 1900	Smee
55	17	1900.240	Red stone pipe bowl inlaid with lead: wooden stem, carved with animals, and painted. L. 71 cm.	”	c. 1900	S. C. Freer
56	17	2563	Red stone pipe bowl; wooden stem with projections near mouthpiece. L. 89.5 cm.	Plains, Quapaw	c. 1860	H. Christy

Cat. No.	Plate No.	Reg. No.	Description	Cultural and tribal or geographical location	Date	Collection
57	17	D.c.90	Red stone pipe bowl: spiral wooden stem. L. 96 cm.	Plains, Sioux	c. 1860	W. Bragge
58	18	D.c.42	Black stone pipe bowl with human head facing recumbent woman. L. 11.25 cm.	Plains, Pawnee?	c. 1850	,,
59	18	D.c.46	Red stone pipe bowl copying a European clay pipe, but with fluted sides. L. 19.5 cm.	Plains	c. 1860	,,
60	18	1853.4–12.169	Unfinished blank for a red stone pipe. L. 13 cm.	Plains, Sioux?	c. 1835	Dr S. Foot
61	18	D.c.55	Unpolished red stone pipe carved with a beaver. L. 12.5 cm.	Plains	c. 1860	W. Bragge
62	19	D.c.76	Pipe tomahawk with screw fitted bowl and spear point: blade engraved with scene of Indian threatening white man on one side, and coat of arms on reverse. L. 31 cm.	Eastern Woodlands	c. 1800	,,
63	19	1878.11–1.627	Pipe tomahawk. L. 40 cm.	,,	c. 1800	Sir Samuel Rush Meyrick
64	19	D.c.72	Pipe tomahawk, British manufacture; type traded by the Hudson's Bay Company. L. 55.5 cm.	,,	c. 1800	W. Bragge
65	19	NN	Pipe tomahawk with engraved brass blade and steel cutting edge; English manufacture, type used in American War of Independence. L. 65 cm.	,,	c. 1780–1830	A. W. Franks
66	20	1900–239	Red stone pipe tomahawk, spontoon form, in two parts joined with wooden tube. L. 46 cm.	Plains, Sioux	c. 1895	S. C. Freer

Cat. No.	Plate No.	Reg. No.	Description	Cultural and tribal or geographical location	Date	Collection
67	20	D.c. 68	Spontoon pipe tomahawk decorated with clusters of quill-wrapped feathers. L. 50 cm.	Eastern Woodlands, Iroquois	c. 1850	W. Bragge
68	20	D.c. 75	Pipe tomahawk: stem decorated with cut-out silver bands and lozenges. L. 54 cm.	Shawnee	c. 1850	„
69	20	1900.278	Pipe tomahawk: stem carved with alligators. L. 54 cm.	Plains, Apache	c. 1880	S. C. Freer
70	21	+5339	Black stone pipe bowl: beaver; eyes inlaid with *Haliotis*. L. 8 cm.	Northwest Coast	19th c.	H. Christy
71	21	2277	Black stone pipe bowl: mythological character. L. 9 cm.	„	19th c.	„
72	21	1976. Am. 3.24	Black stone pipe bowl: whale chasing a seal. H. 8 cm.	„	19th c.	R. B. Inverarity
73	21	D.e. 4	Black stone pipe bowl: bird and mammal. Inlaid with *Haliotis*. L. 11 cm.	„	19th c.	W. Bragge
74	21	1924.3	Black stone pipe: human holding a box. L. 8 cm.	Northwest Coast, Nootka?	c. 1820	J. W. Murphy
75	22	D.e. 5	Argillite pipe of traditional mythological form. L. 46 cm.	Northwest Coast, Haida	c. 1850	W. Bragge
76	22	S. 719	Argillite pipe of traditional mythological form. L. 46 cm.	„	c. 1850	H. Christy
77	22	NN	Argillite pipe of traditional mythological form. L. 50 cm.	„	c. 1850	„
78	24	1954. W. Am. 5.999	Argillite pipe with design of European-Americans, house and dog; inlaid with bone and ivory. L. 35 cm.	„	c. 1860	H. Wellcome

Cat. No.	Plate No.	Reg. No.	Description	Cultural and tribal or geographical location	Date	Collection
79	24	D.c. 22	Argillite pipe with design of European-Americans, dog and house. L. 35.5 cm.	,,	c. 1860	W. Bragge
80	24	D.c. 23	Argillite pipe with design of European floral motifs, thistles and oak leaves, European-Americans, ships rigging and sea monster (?) L. 45 cm.	,,	c. 1840	,,
81	25	1949. Am. 22. NN	Argillite pipe: man with bird; eyes inlaid with *Haliotis*. L. 11 cm.	,,	c. 1860	W. Oldman
82	25	1837.4-8.2	Argillite pipe of traditional mythological form. L. 16.5 cm.	,,	c. 1837	Messrs Brooks and Hedges
83	25	D.c. 39	Argillite pipe copying European clay pipe. L. 13.5 cm.	,,	c. 1840	W. Bragge
84	25	1572	Argillite pipe of clay pipe form carved with European and dog. L. 27 cm.	,,	c. 1840	H. Christy
85	25	1976. Am. 3.74	Argillite pipe of clay pipe form carved with human and an animal. L. 24 cm.	,,	20th c.	R. B. Inverarity
86	26	1949. Am. 22.72	Wooden pipe: inlaid with *Haliotis*; with cylindrical iron bowl. L. 9 cm.	,,	19th c.	W. Oldman
87	26	D.c. 40	Wooden pipe bowl: copying European clay pipe. L. 11.5 cm.	,,	c. 1840	W. Bragge
88	20	6765	Wooden pipe: human surmounted with double-headed serpent, inlaid with *Haliotis*. L. 16.5 cm.	Northwest Coast, Nootka?	19th c.	H. Christy
89	26	1949. Am. 22.79	Wooden pipe: traditional mythological figures inlaid with ivory and *Haliotis*; copper rim to sheet iron bowl. L. 16.5 cm.	Northwest Coast	19th c.	W. Oldman

Cat. No.	Plate No.	Reg. No.	Description	Cultural and tribal or geographical location	Date	Collection
90	26	1949. Am. 22.80	Wooden pipe: wolf; inlaid with *Haliotis*; copper rim to bowl. 15 cm.	Northwest Coast	19th c.	W. Oldman
91	26	D.e.33	Wooden pipe bowl decorated with two European houses; inlaid with bone, ivory, and painted red and green L. 42 cm.	Northwest Coast, Haida	c.1840	W. Bragge
92	27	1900.198	Black stone pipe bowl. L. 7 cm.	California, Modoc	c.1870	S. C. Freer
93	27	1900.151	Orange stone pipe bowl finished with lead. L. 9.25 cm.	Plateau, Molala	c.1870	”
94	27	1900.146	Black stone pipe bowl finished with lead. L. 8 cm.	Plateau, Kliketat	c.1870	”
95	27	Van 167	Green stone smoking tube bound with sinew at the waist of the stem. L. 8.75 cm.	California	c.1792	A. W. Franks
96	28	2572	Grey brown pipe bowl with carved projections and base, with wooden stem. L. 19 cm.	Subarctic, Athabascan	c.1837	H. Christy
97	28	D.c.31	Black stone pipe bowl with silver mount attached by silver chain; bone mouthpiece. L. 21 cm.	Subarctic or Eastern Woodlands, Chippewa or Chippewyan?	c.1860	W. Bragge
98	28	6904 and 6905	Black stone pipe bowl with wooden stem. L. 24 cm.	Subarctic, Chippewyan	c.1860	H. Christy
99	28	1949. Am. 22.29	Walrus ivory pipe with bowl of copper and lead. The stem engraved with scenes of hunting land and sea mammals. L. 24 cm.	Western Eskimo	c.1880	W. Oldman
100	28	B.f.5	Walrus ivory pipe: carved with land mammals and a human shooting; geometric engraving on side, three wooden panels on bottom. L. 33 cm.	”	c.1870	W. Bragge

Plates

The pipes are numbered from left to right and top to bottom in the illustrations

Hopewell pipes from Ohio. Numbers 1–5.

Hopewell pipes from Ohio. Numbers 6–10.

Hopewell pipes from Ohio. Numbers 11–15.

Mississippian effigy pipes. Numbers 16, 17.

Mississippian effigy pipe. Number 18.

Mississippian pipes. Numbers 19–23.

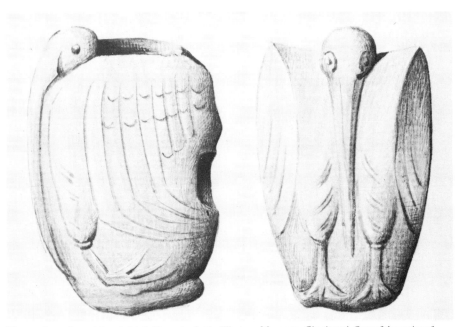

Watercolour of a prehistoric bird effigy pipe in the Western Museum, Cincinatti. One of the series of illustrations executed for W. Bragge 1860–80.

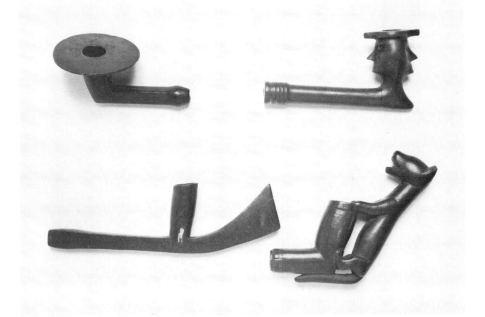

Early historical pipes from Eastern North America. Numbers 24–27.

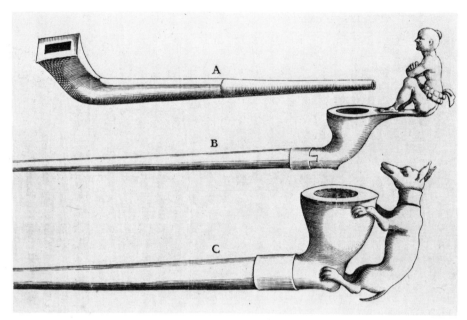

Engraving of three early historical pipes from the Eastern Woodlands. From the plate opposite page 332 in J. Neander: *Traicté du Tabac:* Lyon, 1625. 'A' is a stone pipe, 'B' and 'C' are made of wood.

Iroquois and Micmac pipes. Numbers 28–31.

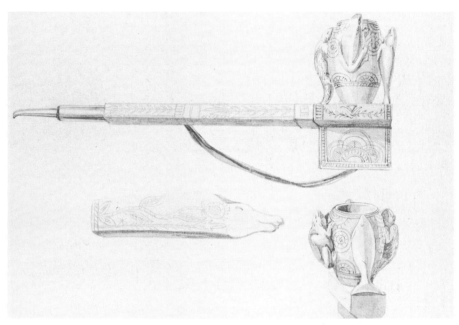

Drawing of a Micmac pipe, profile of the pipe and also a knife handle. Plate 57 of L. L. Hawkins: *Illustrated Gleanings of Aboriginal Ornament from the International Exhibition of 1862*

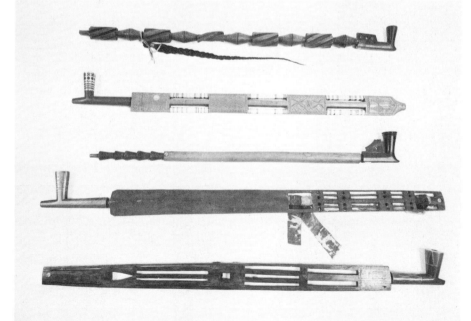

Calumets from the Great Lakes and Eastern Plains. Numbers 32–36.

Pipe bowls from the Great Lakes. Numbers 37–42.

PLATE 14   51

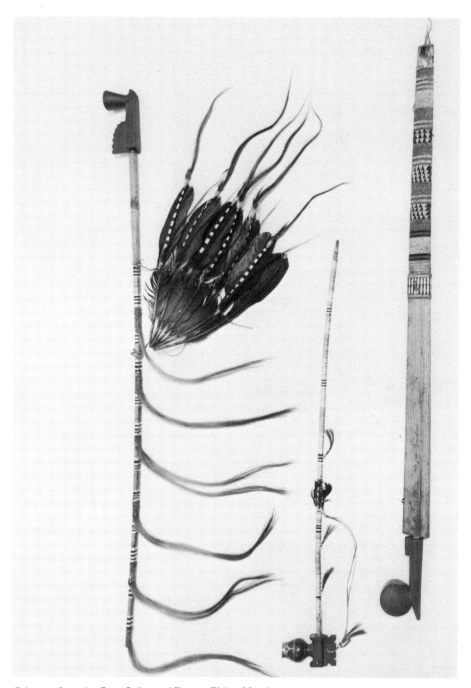

Calumets from the Great Lakes and Eastern Plains. Numbers 43–45.

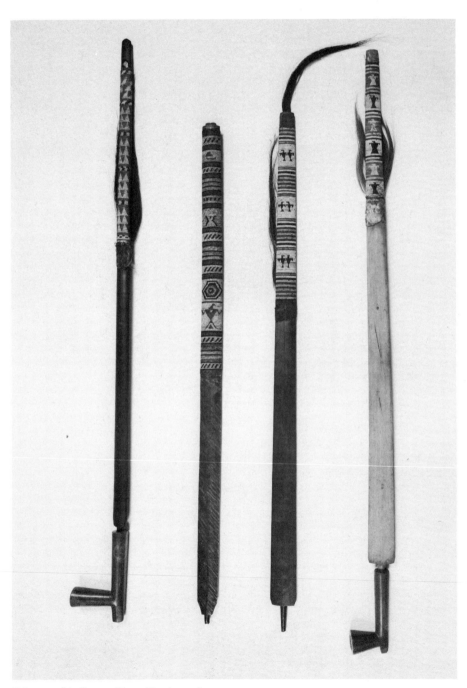

Calumets of the Eastern Sioux. Numbers 46–49.

PLATE 16

53

Calumets of the Plains. Numbers 50–53.

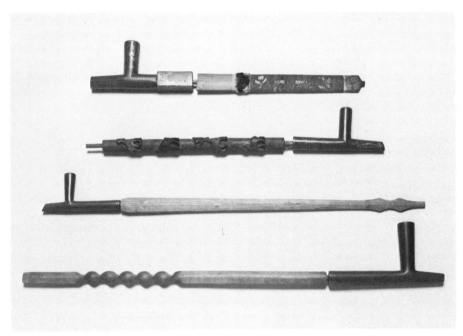

Calumets of the Plains. Numbers 54–57.

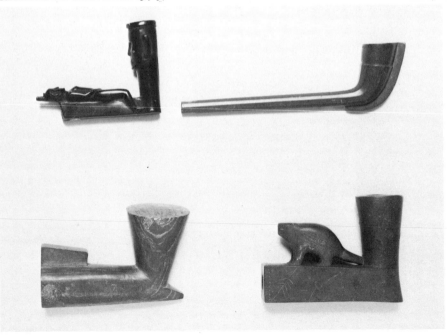

Pipe bowls of the Plains. Numbers 58–61.

PLATE 19   55

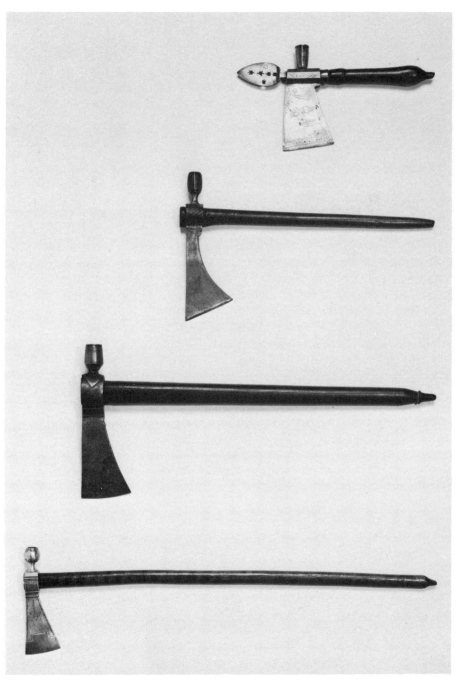

Pipe tomahawks, 1780–1830. Numbers 62–65.

PLATE 20

Pipe tomahawks, 1830–1900. Numbers 66–69.

Stone pipe bowls of the Northwest Coast. Numbers 70–74.

Haida argillite pipes carved with traditional subjects. Numbers 75–77.

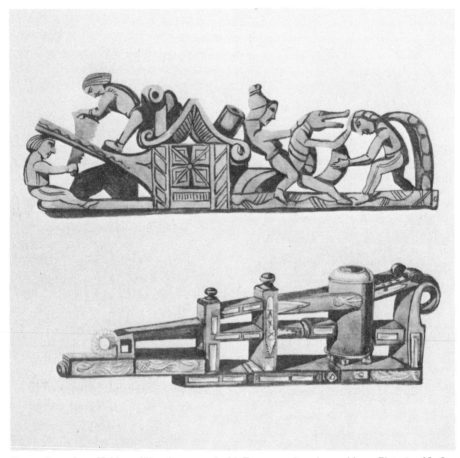

Watercolour of two Haida argillite pipes carved with European-American subjects. Plate 65 of L. L. Hawkins: *Illustrated Gleanings of Aboriginal Ornament*. The subject of the top pipe is described by Hawkins:

'The subject is historical (though not of high cast) the story is clearly told and represents the difficulties of Colonization in a swampy situation.'

The scene probably represents European-American sailors or traders mending a ship or building a house.

PLATE 24

59

Haida argillite pipes carved with European-American subjects. Numbers 78–80.

PLATE 25

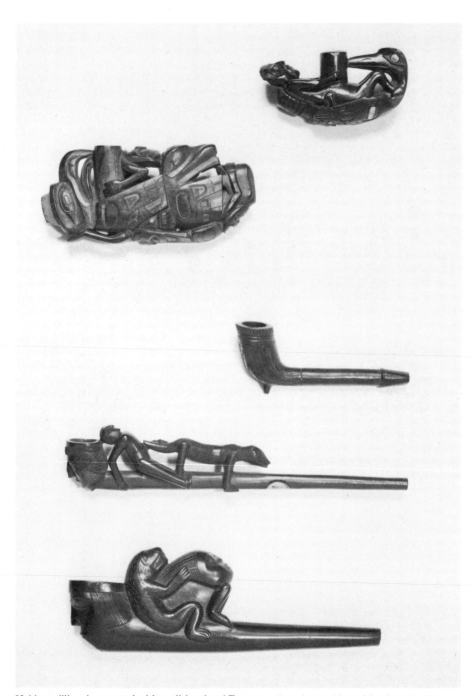

Haida argillite pipes carved with traditional and European-American subjects. Numbers 81–85.

PLATE 26

61

Wooden pipes of the Northwest Coast of traditional and European-American subjects. Numbers 86–91.

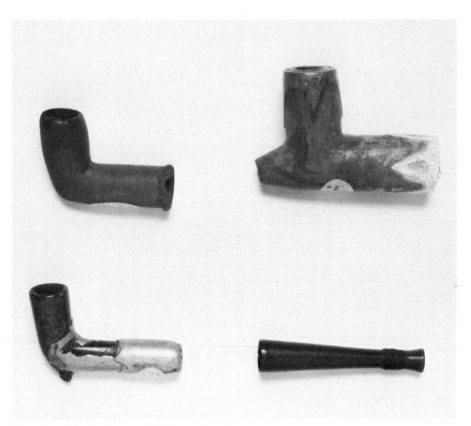

Stone pipes from the Plateau and California. Numbers 92–95.

PLATE 28   63

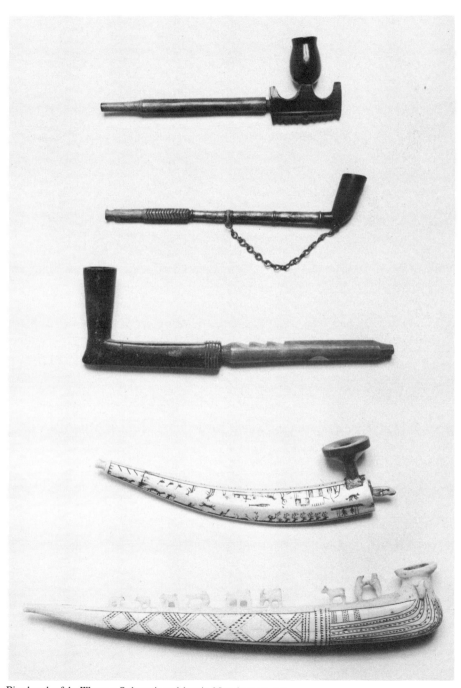

Pipe bowls of the Western Subarctic and Arctic. Numbers 96–100.